Collins

Key Stage 3
Hinduism

Tristan Elby
Series Editor: Robert Orme

HarperCollins
PUBLISHERS
Since 1817

William Collins' dream of knowledge for all began with the publication of his first book in 1819. A self-educated mill worker, he not only enriched millions of lives, but also founded a flourishing publishing house. Today, staying true to this spirit, Collins books are packed with inspiration, innovation and practical expertise. They place you at the centre of a world of possibility and give you exactly what you need to explore it.

Collins. Freedom to teach

Published by Collins
An imprint of HarperCollins*Publishers*
The News Building
1 London Bridge Street
London SE1 9GF

HarperCollins *Publishers*
1st Floor
Watermarque Building
Ringsend Road
Dublin 4
Ireland

Publisher: Joanna Ramsay
Editor: Hannah Dove
Author: Tristan Elby
Series Editor: Robert Orme
Development Editor: Sonya Newland
Project manager: Emily Hooton
Copy-editor: Jill Morris
Image researcher: Shelley Noronha
Proof-reader: Ros and Chris Davies
Cover designer: We Are Laura
Cover image: robert stoetzel/Alamy
Production controller: Rachel Weaver
Typesetter: QBS

MIX
Paper from
responsible sources
FSC˙ C007454

FSC™ is a non-profit international organisation established to promote the responsible management of the world's forests. Products carrying the FSC label are independently certified to assure consumers that they come from forests that are managed to meet the social, economic and ecological needs of present and future generations, and other controlled sources.

Find out more about HarperCollins and the environment at
www.harpercollins.co.uk/green

Printed and Bound in the UK using 100% Renewable Electricity at CPI Group (UK) Ltd

Contents

INTRODUCTION 4

UNIT 1: History and belief 6

1.1 What is Hinduism? 8

1.2 Hindu gods and goddesses 10

1.3 How do Hindus use symbols? 12

1.4 Sacred texts 14

1.5 Karma, samsara and moksha 16

1.6 Dharma 18

1.7 What is yoga? 20

1.8 Extraordinary individuals 22

Knowledge organiser 24

UNIT 2: Hinduism in the modern world 26

2.1 Forms and places of worship 28

2.2 Places of pilgrimage 30

2.3 Hindu festivals 32

2.4 What is the caste system? 34

2.5 Hindu attitudes to violence 36

2.6 Do Hindus believe in gender equality? 38

2.7 What are Hindu attitudes to the environment? 40

2.8 Hinduism in world culture 42

Knowledge organiser 44

INDEX 46

ACKNOWLEDGEMENTS 48

Introduction

It is not easy to define what makes something a religion. In some religions one god is worshipped, in others many gods are worshipped, and in some no god is worshipped at all. Some religions have a single founder. In others, there is not one person who starts it or one clear moment when it began. To make things more complicated, there are often strong differences of opinion between and even within particular religions. Two people following the same religion can believe opposing things and follow their religion in strikingly different ways. Within any religion, some people build their whole lives around their beliefs while others are less committed to their religion but still think of themselves as part of it. Followers of all religions believe that they have found truth, but their ideas about what is true differ greatly.

Approximately 84 per cent of people in the world today follow a religion and experts predict that this will rise to 87 per cent by 2050. The most followed religion in the UK is Christianity, but there are also followers of many other religions including Islam, Judaism, Buddhism, Hinduism and Sikhism. In recent times there has also been a big increase in the number of people in the UK who do not follow any religion. Some are atheists which means that they do not believe there is a god or gods. Others are agnostics meaning they are not sure if a god or gods exist. Others might believe there is a god or gods, but choose not to belong to a religion.

By studying the beliefs and ways of life of millions of people around the world, you will gain a greater understanding of the past, the modern world and humanity itself. You will explore questions that have troubled humankind through the ages and examine the diverse ways in which these questions have been answered. In a world where religion has and continues to play such a large role, the importance of understanding it is as great as ever.

Robert Orme (Series Editor)

Concise topic introductions set the scene and focus your learning.

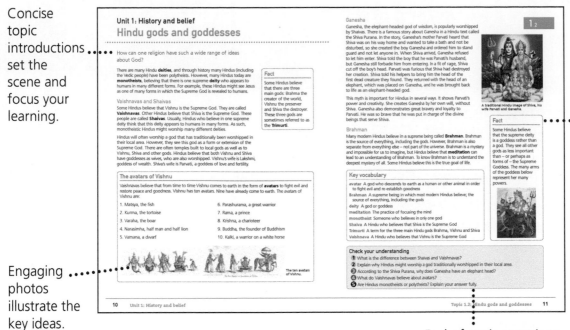

Fact boxes provide bite-sized details.

Engaging photos illustrate the key ideas.

End-of-topic questions are designed to check and consolidate your understanding.

Key fact boxes help you to revise and remember the main points from each unit.

Key vocabulary lists for each unit help you define and remember important terms.

Key people boxes summarise the key figures from the unit.

Knowledge organisers can be used to revise and quiz yourself on key dates, definitions and descriptions.

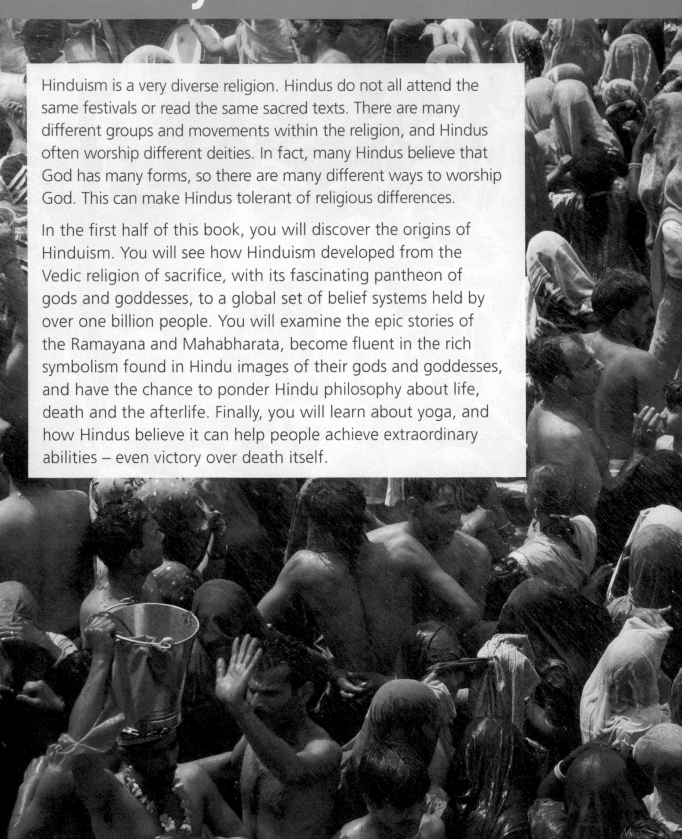

History and belief

Hinduism is a very diverse religion. Hindus do not all attend the same festivals or read the same sacred texts. There are many different groups and movements within the religion, and Hindus often worship different deities. In fact, many Hindus believe that God has many forms, so there are many different ways to worship God. This can make Hindus tolerant of religious differences.

In the first half of this book, you will discover the origins of Hinduism. You will see how Hinduism developed from the Vedic religion of sacrifice, with its fascinating pantheon of gods and goddesses, to a global set of belief systems held by over one billion people. You will examine the epic stories of the Ramayana and Mahabharata, become fluent in the rich symbolism found in Hindu images of their gods and goddesses, and have the chance to ponder Hindu philosophy about life, death and the afterlife. Finally, you will learn about yoga, and how Hindus believe it can help people achieve extraordinary abilities – even victory over death itself.

1.1	What is Hinduism?	8
1.2	Hindu gods and goddesses	10
1.3	How do Hindus use symbols?	12
1.4	Sacred texts	14
1.5	Karma, samsara and moksha	16
1.6	Dharma	18
1.7	What is yoga?	20
1.8	Extraordinary individuals	22
Knowledge organiser		24

What is Hinduism?

The ancient religion of Hinduism has over one billion followers today, but do all Hindus share the same beliefs?

Various aspects of the religion that we call Hinduism can be traced to India over 3000 years ago. This makes it one of the oldest religions in the world, and the oldest of the six major world religions. Today, Hinduism is the third-largest religion in the world, with over a billion followers worldwide, known as Hindus. The word 'Hindu' comes from a river called the Indus that flowed through the area of northwest India where Hinduism developed. Most Hindus still live in India, but the religion has also spread to other countries. There are more than 800,000 Hindus living in Britain.

The Indus river in Ladakh, India.

A diverse religion

Unlike many other religions, there was not one person who founded Hinduism, nor was there one specific moment when it began. There is no single powerful leader or group of leaders in Hinduism. Hindus have many different beliefs and they do not all worship the same gods and goddesses. Some people have even described Hinduism as a collection of many different religions rather than one religion.

There is no one book that tells Hindus what to believe or how to live; there are many different books that Hindus can choose to read, or not. However, Hindus view the four **Vedas** as sacred. These are the oldest Hindu texts and, like many other Hindu books, they are written in **Sanskrit**. The Vedas tell us what Hindus believed and how they worshipped 3000 years ago.

What was Vedic Hinduism like?

The Vedas mention a large number of gods and goddesses, and the Vedic people were **polytheistic**. Many of the Vedic gods were in charge of parts of the natural world that were useful or potentially dangerous to the Vedic people. For example, Rudra was a much-feared god who inflicted illness upon farm animals if he was unhappy with the way people were worshipping him. Indra was the god of sky, who sent thunderbolts to earth. People also worshipped gods of the sun, earth, fire and dawn.

Fact

The first of the four Vedas, the Rig Veda, says 'Let noble thoughts come to us from all directions.' This shows that Hindus should welcome good ideas wherever they come from and that they are comfortable with diversity. One Hindu hymn compares different religions or paths to God with hundreds of different streams and rivers, which ultimately end up in the same ocean. Many Hindus today believe that other religious beliefs may be equally true, and they do not try to convert others to Hinduism.

These Vedic gods were deeply relevant to life in ancient India, where a bad harvest or the premature death of animals could spell disaster for people who depended on these things. As Hinduism spread and society developed, Hindus began to change the gods and goddesses they worshipped. However, most Vedic deities still have a place in Hindu symbolism and worship today.

Indra, the king of the Vedic gods, riding his three-headed elephant. In his hand is an object that represents his weapon – a thunderbolt.

Animal sacrifice

One way in which the Vedic people tried to keep their gods happy was through the **sacrifice** of food and animals. The Vedas refer to sacrifices of goats, oxen and even horses. This would have been done on a special sacrificial altar sometimes in the shape

A Vedic fire altar. These are still used for sacrifices in some parts of the world.

of a falcon or eagle. Agni (the god of fire, also the Sanskrit word for fire) consumed the food offered in the sacrifice. This made it acceptable to the gods.

Vedic Hindus believed that gods and humans helped each other. Humans offered the gods food and animals in order to please them, and in return they believed that the gods would send good weather, fine crops and keep their animals healthy. For this reason, Agni was a very important god, because the sacrifices he made possible caused the gods to rain blessings down on earth.

Over time, animal sacrifice gradually became a lot less popular, but it does still exist among Hindus in some parts of the world.

How did Hinduism develop?

One reason why Hinduism is so diverse today is because it developed among many different people over a long period of time and across a very large area. Different people had different ideas in different places at different times. The Hinduism that exists today is the result of a long process of change and development over 3000 years. In the following pages, you will learn more about this journey.

Key vocabulary

polytheistic Referring to belief in many gods; someone who believes in many gods is a polytheist

sacrifice A method of worship that involves offering animals or food to the gods

Sanskrit A language used in ancient India, which many Hindu texts are written in

Vedas A collection of sacred writings, literally meaning 'knowledge'

Check your understanding

1. When and where did Hinduism begin?
2. What are Hindu sacred texts called and in what language were they written?
3. Explain at least two differences between Vedic religion and modern Hinduism.
4. Why is there so much diversity in Hinduism today?
5. How is Hinduism different from one other religion that you have studied?

Unit 1: History and belief
Hindu gods and goddesses

How can one religion have such a wide range of ideas about God?

There are many Hindu **deities**, and through history many Hindus (including the Vedic people) have been polytheists. However, many Hindus today are **monotheists**, believing that there is one supreme **deity** who appears to humans in many different forms. For example, these Hindus might see Jesus as one of many forms in which the Supreme God is revealed to humans.

Vaishnavas and Shaivas

Some Hindus believe that Vishnu is the Supreme God. They are called **Vaishnavas**. Other Hindus believe that Shiva is the Supreme God. These people are called **Shaivas**. Usually, Hindus who believe in one supreme deity think that this deity appears to humans in many forms. As such, monotheistic Hindus might worship many different deities.

Hindus will often worship a god that has traditionally been worshipped in their local area. However, they see this god as a form or extension of the Supreme God. There are often temples built to local gods as well as to Vishnu, Shiva and other gods. Hindus believe that both Vishnu and Shiva have goddesses as wives, who are also worshipped. Vishnu's wife is Lakshmi, goddess of wealth. Shiva's wife is Parvati, a goddess of love and fertility.

> ## Fact
>
> Some Hindus believe that there are three main gods: Brahma the creator of the world, Vishnu the preserver and Shiva the destroyer. These three gods are sometimes referred to as the **Trimurti**.

The avatars of Vishnu

Vaishnavas believe that from time to time Vishnu comes to earth in the form of **avatars** to fight evil and restore peace and goodness. Vishnu has ten avatars. Nine have already come to earth. The avatars of Vishnu are:

1. Matsya, the fish
2. Kurma, the tortoise
3. Varaha, the boar
4. Narasimha, half man and half lion
5. Vamana, a dwarf

6. Parashurama, a great warrior
7. Rama, a prince
8. Krishna, a charioteer
9. Buddha, the founder of Buddhism
10. Kalki, a warrior on a white horse

The ten avatars of Vishnu.

Ganesha

Ganesha, the elephant-headed god of wisdom, is popularly worshipped by Shaivas. There is a famous story about Ganesha in a Hindu text called the Shiva Purana. In the story, Ganesha's mother Parvati heard that Shiva was on his way home and wanted to take a bath and not be disturbed, so she created the boy Ganesha and ordered him to stand guard and not let anyone in. When Shiva arrived, Ganesha refused to let him enter. Shiva told the boy that he was Parvati's husband, but Ganesha still forbade him from entering. In a fit of rage, Shiva cut off the boy's head. Parvati was furious that Shiva had destroyed her creation. Shiva told his helpers to bring him the head of the first dead creature they found. They returned with the head of an elephant, which was placed on Ganesha, and he was brought back to life as an elephant-headed god.

This myth is important for Hindus in several ways. It shows Parvati's power and creativity. She creates Ganesha by her own will, without Shiva. Ganesha also demonstrates great bravery and loyalty to Parvati. He was so brave that he was put in charge of the divine beings that serve Shiva.

A traditional Hindu image of Shiva, his wife Parvati and Ganesha.

Brahman

Many modern Hindus believe in a supreme being called **Brahman**. Brahman is the source of everything, including the gods. However, Brahman is also separate from everything else – not part of the universe. Brahman is a mystery and impossible for us to imagine, but Hindus believe that **meditation** can lead to an understanding of Brahman. To know Brahman is to understand the deepest mystery of all. Some Hindus believe this is the true goal of life.

Fact

Some Hindus believe that the supreme deity is a goddess rather than a god. They see all other gods as less important than – or perhaps as forms of – the Supreme Goddess. The many arms of the goddess below represent her many powers.

Key vocabulary

avatar A god who descends to earth as a human or other animal in order to fight evil and re-establish goodness

Brahman A supreme being in which most modern Hindus believe; the source of everything, including the gods

deity A god or goddess

meditation The practice of focusing the mind

monotheist Someone who believes in only one god

Shaiva A Hindu who believes that Shiva is the Supreme God

Trimurti A term for the three main Hindu gods Brahma, Vishnu and Shiva

Vaishnava A Hindu who believes that Vishnu is the Supreme God

Check your understanding

1 What is the difference between Shaivas and Vaishnavas?

2 Explain why Hindus might worship a god traditionally worshipped in their local area.

3 According to the Shiva Purana, why does Ganesha have an elephant head?

4 What do Vaishnavas believe about avatars?

5 Are Hindus monotheists or polytheists? Explain your answer fully.

Unit 1: History and belief
How do Hindus use symbols?

What are the secrets of Hindu symbols?

Vishnu

Hindu deities are often shown as having several arms. This is to symbolise that gods and goddesses have superior powers to humans. In the picture below, Vishnu has four arms. This may represent the four directions of the compass, showing that Vishnu is the supreme ruler of the universe who rules in all directions. Vishnu is also holding a different object in each of his hands. These objects are all Hindu **symbols**.

The round object is a **chakra** ('wheel'), which is a hugely powerful divine weapon. When someone throws a chakra, it returns, so it symbolises Vishnu's power, which cannot be exhausted.

In this hand, Vishnu holds a conch shell. Conches produce a distinctive sound when blown, so this could represent both the breath of life that the god breathes into living things and the sacred sound **Aum** (or Om) that Hindus chant.

The flower Vishnu holds is a lotus, which can represent purity. It can also symbolise Lakshmi, his wife, who gives him his energy. Some Hindus see the lotus flower as representing detachment, which means not getting too attached to the pleasures or opportunities life brings.

In this hand, Vishnu holds a powerful, heavy weapon called a mace. This symbolises the way that Vishnu sometimes takes a physical form (avatar) in order to fight evil.

Shiva

The picture of Shiva is a good example of a single image containing a great deal of symbolism. Shiva has his legs crossed, as if meditating. Shiva is highly praised for his ability to sit absorbed in perfect meditation. Hindus often meditate in simple, remote locations, and here Shiva is sitting on Mount Kailash, a sacred and legendary mountain where many Hindus believe he and his wife Parvati live. The god is wearing a simple animal skin, just as someone who has dedicated himself to meditation would.

Hindus believe that meditation can bring great powers. The three white lines on Shiva's forehead are called the **vibhuti**. This symbol represents his superhuman powers and the fact that he is everywhere in the universe. At the centre of Shiva's forehead is his 'third eye'. This represents the wisdom that Shiva has gained through meditation.

Shiva sitting in meditation.

The bull standing behind Shiva is called Nandi. Hindu deities usually have what is known as a **vahana**, a vehicle, so that they can travel around, and a deity's vahana will usually appear alongside him or her in images. Bulls are strong and dedicated, just as Shiva is strong and dedicated to doing good. However, bulls are also independent and headstrong, so the bull can also suggest that Shiva is a slightly wild, untamed god. Nandi the bull can also represent a devoted follower of Shiva.

Vishnu has a mace as a weapon, whereas Shiva has a trident, called a **trishula**. Some Hindus believe that, at the end of time, Shiva will destroy the universe with this weapon so that it can be created again.

Snake symbols

If you look closely at the images on these pages, you can see a snake in the ocean underneath Vishnu and another around Shiva's neck. The snake near Vishnu could be a symbol of infinity – a snake that is infinitely long, just as Vishnu is infinitely powerful. It could also refer to a Hindu myth about Vasuki, the king of serpents. In this myth, the gods use Vasuki to churn the ocean in order to extract a liquid that would grant immortality. The churning also produces a poison, which Shiva drinks from the mouth of Vasuki in order to save others, so the snake around his neck could represent this.

Sculpture of Shiva sitting in meditation on Ganges river in Rishikesh, India, 2011.

Key vocabulary

Aum A sacred syllable or sound that is very important to Hindus and which they chant

chakra A word meaning 'wheel', one of the weapons that Hindu gods may carry

symbol An image that expresses religious ideas

trishula A word meaning 'three spears', another weapon symbolising the power and authority of the gods

vahana An animal 'vehicle' that transports Hindu deities

vibhuti The three white lines on Shiva's forehead, which represent his superhuman powers

Check your understanding

1. What is a symbol?
2. What could Vishnu's four arms represent?
3. Explain which symbols in the picture of Shiva refer to meditation.
4. Explain what the weapons of Shiva and Vishnu might symbolise for Hindus.
5. Explain, with examples, why symbols are important in Hinduism.

Unit 1: History and belief
Sacred texts

Where did Hindu texts come from and what is in them?

The Vedas

Nearly all Hindus agree that the four Vedas are sacred and revealed by God. The Vedas contain hymns to Hindu gods and goddesses as well as teachings about the soul and the afterlife, and detailed instructions on how to worship and perform rituals.

The Vedas are sometimes called **shruti**, which literally means 'heard', because this is how Hindus believe the Vedas were first received. The Vedic people who received the Vedas were called **Rishis**. They were great meditators and this allowed them to see and hear things that ordinary humans could not. After the Rishis 'heard' the Vedas, they taught them to priests, who memorised and recited them to the next generation. This continued for many centuries. Hindus believe that the Vedas were passed on so accurately that they are almost like a recording of what people were reciting 3000 years ago.

The Mahabharata and the Ramayana

There are other holy or sacred texts in Hinduism. Among the oldest are two epic stories known as the **Mahabharata** and the **Ramayana**. Each of these is a very long story made up of many shorter stories.

The Ramayana is about a warrior called King Rama and his beautiful wife Sita. The story tells of how a terrifying demon king called Ravana kidnapped Sita because he wanted her to be his wife. In his search for Sita, Rama came across Hanuman, king of the monkeys, who agreed to help him. A message was passed to all the monkeys in the world to find Sita. The monkeys passed the message on to the bears, who were led by their king, Jambavan. Eventually, Hanuman found Sita imprisoned on the island of Lanka. A wise monkey called Nala assisted Hanuman by building a huge bridge to Lanka. In the battle to rescue Sita, Rama killed Ravana with a magic arrow. As Rama and Sita returned home to the city of Ayodhya, people lit lights to guide them and welcome them back.

The Ramayana is inspiring for Hindus because it gives examples of good Hindu behaviour. Hanuman shows great loyalty to Rama by helping him, while Sita is a brave, loyal wife who does not give up hope that Rama will rescue her. The story also has an inspirational message that good defeats evil.

> **Fact**
>
> Many scholars of Hinduism believe that the process of composing the Vedas began around 1500 BCE, and it probably took almost a thousand years for all four Vedas to be composed.

Part of the Rig Veda written in Sanskrit.

Sita being abducted by the many-armed demon Ravana.

The Mahabharata is a tale of a devastating war between two sides of the same family. It contains so many smaller stories that it spans several volumes and is more than twice as long as the Christian Bible. Most Hindus do not read all of the Mahabharata, but many find a small part of it called the Bhagavad Gita ('The Song of the Lord') particularly inspiring. In the Bhagavad Gita, a conversation takes place on a battlefield between a warrior called Arjuna and his charioteer, Krishna, an avatar of Vishnu. At first, Arjuna does not realise that Krishna is an avatar. As they talk, Krishna tells Arjuna how to live a good life, how people should live together in society and what happens after death. Krishna then reveals his true form to Arjuna. Arjuna is overwhelmed that he has seen and talked to God.

The Puranas

Even after the Vedas were complete, many Hindus continued to compose sacred texts. These are known as the **Puranas**, which means 'ancient ones'. Hindus who worship Vishnu consider the Bhagavata Purana to be a very holy text. It teaches about the need to show Vishnu complete devotion. Other Puranas describe what the end of the current age will be like. They predict that the world will be very chaotic and there will be much evil. Some Vaishnavas believe that at this time Vishnu will take the form of Kalki, a warrior on a white horse holding a blazing sword. Kalki will fight a war against the forces of evil, which will end in a great battle against two demon generals. All evil will be destroyed, marking the start of a new golden age.

Different Hindu communities recite or celebrate different texts because they focus on different gods or goddesses.

Key vocabulary

Mahabharata An epic story that is inspirational for Hindus

Purana A Hindu text that is more recent than the Vedas, but is still thought to contain profound wisdom and teachings

Ramayana An epic story that is inspirational for Hindus

Rishis The Vedic people who first heard the Vedas and taught them to others

shruti A word referring to religious teachings that are revealed to Rishis directly from God

Check your understanding

1. Why are the Vedas sometimes called 'shruti'?
2. When were the Vedas written and how long did this process take?
3. Explain what happens in the Ramayana and why Hindus find it inspiring.
4. Explain what happens in the Bhagavad Gita and why Hindus find it inspiring.
5. What are the Puranas and what might they teach Hindus?

Unit 1: History and belief
Karma, samsara and moksha

How do Hindus believe that their next lives will be decided?

Samsara

Hindus believe that their current life is just one of many lives they have already led and will lead in the future. They believe that when a person dies his or her soul is reborn in a new body. This will not necessarily be a human body – the person's next life could be as an animal, an insect or a species completely unknown to us.

A person's next life depends on **karma**. Good deeds store up good karma and bad deeds store up bad karma. Depending on a person's actions, he or she might be **reincarnated** as any type of creature, or even find him or herself in heaven or hell. All these reincarnations are temporary.

Samsara is a Sanskrit word that Hindus use to describe the continual journey of the soul through many reincarnations. Samsara also refers to the universe within which these reincarnations take place. Hindus believe that we are all journeying through samsara, and have been for billions of years.

For Hindus, good deeds, such as this woman donating food, store up good karma.

Moksha

Hindus believe that people can have many positive experiences within samsara, and many fulfilling lives. However, there will also be a large number of painful and unpleasant lives, although people tend to forget each life as they move to the next one.

To break this cycle, Hindus want to achieve **moksha** – a permanent escape from samsara.

It is difficult to describe moksha. Because samsara is essentially the whole universe, moksha is completely unlike anything people have experienced in any of their lives. Generally, however, achieving moksha means you are not reborn and do not change any more. There is no further suffering of any kind. Many Hindus believe that moksha will involve everlasting bliss and inner peace. Some believe that moksha involves being united with God forever.

This mural in a palace in India shows the elephant king Gajendra achieving moksha.

Others think that moksha is when you realise that you were never different from God in the first place – all of samsara was just an illusion that made you think that you were separate from God.

Nirvana

Buddhists also believe in karma and samsara and try to achieve freedom from samsara. They call this achieving nirvana or parinirvana. However, Buddhists tend to disagree with Hindus about whether they will be united with God after escaping samsara. Many Buddhists think that nirvana is a state of perfect peace, which will not involve any gods or goddesses at all.

Achieving moksha

Achieving moksha can take many lifetimes. One way of achieving moksha is through yoga (see pages 20–21). People who are excellent at yoga, called yogins, are believed to be able to purify themselves of bad karma. If you meditate and develop your mind and body in the right way, you will eventually be freed from any further reincarnation. Yoga can involve fasting and long and painful exercises. It also requires meditation – focusing the mind completely on God.

Another way of achieving moksha is through **bhakti**, which is Sanskrit for 'devotion' or 'worship'. This involves becoming increasingly devoted to God throughout each of your lifetimes. As your worship and devotion increases, your soul will be purified. Eventually, like the yogins, you will achieve moksha.

This man is trying to achieve moksha through yoga and meditation.

Key vocabulary

bhakti A Sanskrit word meaning 'devotion' or 'worship'; some Hindus believe that bhakti alone can be a way to achieve moksha

karma The forces that influence people's fortune and future reincarnations

moksha Escaping from samsara and never dying or becoming reincarnated again; the word literally means 'release'

reincarnated When a soul is reborn by passing into a new body

samsara The continual process of death and reincarnation; also, the entire universe as we know it

The Upanishads are very old philosophical texts that explain some key Hindu ideas about life after death.

❝ And here is he born either as a grasshopper, or a fish, or a bird, or a lion, or a boar, or a serpent, or a tiger, or a man, or some other creature, according to his deeds and his knowledge. ❞
Kaushitaki Brahmana Upanishad

❝ When a caterpillar has come to the end of a blade of grass, it reaches out to another blade, and draws itself over to it. In the same way the soul, having coming to the end of one life, reaches out to another body, and draws itself over to it. ❞
Brihadaranyaka Upanishad

❝ As a man casts off his worn-out clothes, and takes other new ones in their place, so does the embodied soul cast off his worn-out bodies, and enter others anew. ❞
Bhagavad Gita

Activity

Draw and label three images that illustrate karma, samsara and moksha.

Check your understanding

1 Explain what Hindus mean by reincarnation.
2 How is a soul's next reincarnation decided?
3 What is moksha and why is it difficult to imagine what moksha is like?
4 Describe two ways to achieve moksha.
5 'Karma, reincarnation and moksha do not exist.' Discuss this statement.

Unit 1: History and belief
Dharma

How do people in different situations follow the same universal law of dharma?

In Hinduism, people's thoughts and behaviour store up karma, which affects their next lives. This is one reason why Hindus try to behave morally. When it comes to living a good life, the key idea in Hinduism is **dharma**, which can be broadly translated as 'duty', 'righteousness' or 'moral law'.

Hindus believe that the Supreme Being has revealed dharma to people through sacred texts and that to follow dharma successfully is to achieve their deepest purpose. Following dharma carefully is likely to create good karma and cause a good reincarnation in the next life.

How do you follow dharma?

Everyone follows dharma in different ways. For King Rama, following dharma meant ruling justly and setting a good example for his people. Rama was also a husband whose wife had been kidnapped. In that situation, dharma meant rescuing Sita no matter how dangerous it was. For Sita, dharma meant being loyal to Rama and not giving up hope that she would be rescued. These examples show that following dharma is not always easy.

For many Hindus today, being loyal and respectful to their families and communities would be behaving in accordance with dharma. Giving to charity and showing kindness to those less fortunate is also part of dharma. In the UK, many Hindus support Sewa UK, a Hindu charity that provides help in places of need and supports people with disabilities. This is a very dharmic activity.

Rama, assisted by the monkey army of Hanuman, defeats the demon Ravana. He is upholding dharma by saving his wife and defeating evil, despite the danger.

A Sewa UK charity shop. Helping those in need is part of the Hindu duty of 'sewa' or 'service'.

Dharma in Hindu texts

Dharma is sometimes difficult to follow, and Hindu texts include many examples of people trying hard to follow dharma in difficult situations. In the Bhagavad Gita, Krishna tells Arjuna that he must fight in the war of the Mahabharata because it is righteous. Krishna says that no matter how difficult it might be – even if it means fighting family members – Arjuna must follow dharma by doing his duty as a warrior on the side of goodness and justice.

Stages of life

Hindus believe that ways of following dharma can change depending on your stage of life. For young people, dharma could mean studying hard and respecting their families. From a young age, many Hindu boys 'take the sacred thread'. This is a thin cord that they accept to show that they are ready to learn sacred scriptures like the Vedas. They receive it in a ceremony called the **upanayana**, and they wear the thread for the rest of their lives. Hindus believe that continuing this tradition preserves dharma and pleases God. In earlier times, the tradition was only for boys in the top three classes of society (see pages 34–35). Nowadays, it is more widespread, and girls sometimes receive a similar initiation.

Once Hindus reach adulthood, there are new important parts of dharma. These include marrying, raising children and taking care of their parents, especially when they are elderly.

Eternal dharma

Some Hindus believe in **sanatana dharma**. This means 'eternal' or 'timeless' dharma. The world has changed a lot over the course of history, but for Hindus some things remain the same. Whatever the time and place, showing devotion to God, being loyal to your family and community, and making the best possible use of your talents and situation are always part of dharma.

Hindus believe that God has made sure that the universe is fundamentally good and lawful. Evil and chaos may sometimes seem powerful, but dharma still exists and will eventually be restored. Vaishnavas believe that Vishnu has taken different forms in different times and places, but whether he is a fish, a dwarf or a prince, he still upholds the same eternal dharma.

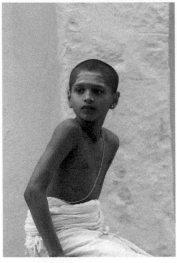

A boy who has taken the sacred thread.

Key vocabulary

dharma The moral law that Hindus must follow; the word can be translated as 'duty' or 'righteousness'

sanatana dharma Eternal dharma or law; this never changes and is always good, regardless of the time and place

upanayana A traditional Hindu ceremony that children undergo when they are ready to be educated about the Vedas and other sacred texts

Check your understanding

1. What does the word 'dharma' mean?
2. What did behaving in accordance with dharma mean for Sita?
3. Describe the two ways that Rama needed to follow dharma in the Ramayana.
4. Explain how dharma changes at different stages of life.
5. Using these pages and page 10, describe how Vishnu upholds dharma.

Unit 1: History and belief
What is yoga?

Can yoga help people escape the cycle of samsara?

What is yoga?

Today, many non-Hindus practise **yoga**, but it has been part of Hinduism for thousands of years. Yoga is a Sanskrit word meaning 'yoke', a harness that is placed on an animal to control it. Through yoga, Hindus try to yoke, or control, their mind and body. Yoga can also mean 'concentration', which is a key part of its practice.

Hindus who perform yoga think that the mind is constantly 'looking around' restlessly, unable to focus on a particular thing. They believe that yoga and meditation help control the mind and body so you are always calm and have a clear mind. This allows you to focus on truly important things and achieve a better reincarnation, or even moksha.

How do you practise yoga?

Asanas – the postures that people move their bodies into – are a key part of yoga. Some are quite simple, but others are very difficult to achieve.

Another part of yoga is pranayama, meaning 'breath control'. Being aware of and in control of your breathing is important in yoga, as it can calm you down and make it easier to concentrate and meditate. Some Hindus believe that people have a spiritual energy or force within them, which can be developed through pranayama.

A third part of yoga is dhyana, meaning 'meditation'. Meditation can involve concentrating on one object without letting anything else distract you, or trying to have no thoughts at all for a long period of time, which is very difficult! Many Hindus believe that for yoga to be successful it needs to involve all three of the elements above. Without meditation, your mind will still be distracted, and you will continue to be reincarnated.

These women are sitting in the 'sukhasana' posture. This is a simple and relatively comfortable position that is good for meditation.

Ascetics

Ascetics are people who have chosen to live their lives without the everyday comforts we are used to. In India, ascetics often live outside, or continually travel from one place to another. They eat only simple food and often fast for long periods. They have few possessions and clothes, and they tend to live by begging. Hindus believe that they can gain good karma by giving ascetics food or other help.

Some Hindu ascetics believe that their lifestyle will generate a lot of **tapas**, which means 'heat' in Sanskrit. Tapas purifies the mind and body.

By fasting intensively or staying in difficult yoga postures for a long time, a person can generate purifying tapas. This purity brings people closer to moksha. Through the ages, many Hindus have taken up yoga and meditation to achieve this.

This Hindu man from India is living as an ascetic. He is practising yoga by adopting a difficult asana, or posture.

> ❝ By meditating on a pure inner light, free from pain, the mind becomes stable and calm. Or by meditating on having no desire for material objects, the mind becomes stable and calm. ❞
>
> From the Yoga Sutras, a short text by the yogin Patanjali

Feature

The legend of Vishvamitra

There are many examples in Hindu myths of men and women who gain extraordinary powers because they follow an ascetic lifestyle. In the Ramayana, a man named Vishvamitra is said to have built up massive power and great abilities by meditating and fasting at the top of the Himalayas. He ate nothing (and barely breathed) for a thousand years as he tried to become a Rishi. Vishvamitra was not always perfect, and he is said to have once used his ascetic powers to turn a beautiful lady into a stone for 10,000 years because she disturbed his meditation! Despite this, Vishvamitra's asceticism led to him being respected as a truly great Rishi. He became famous for using his yogic powers for good, and often helped people in need.

The beautiful Menaka distracts Vishvamitra from his meditation. He was famously irritable and turned her to stone on the spot!

Key vocabulary

ascetic Someone who lives a simple life away from society, usually to become closer to the supreme being or to achieve moksha (also known as a sadhu)

tapas Literally 'heat'; ascetics and people practising yoga intensively generate tapas

yoga Controlling the mind and body to purify yourself and achieve moksha

Check your understanding

1. Explain what the word 'yoga' means and why it is important to Hindus.
2. Describe three parts of yoga.
3. Explain what an ascetic lifestyle involves and why people choose to follow it.
4. How did Vishvamitra use the powers he gained from living an ascetic life?
5. 'The most spiritual life is an ascetic life.' Do you agree?

Unit 1: History and belief
Extraordinary individuals

Who are some of the extraordinary individuals who inspire Hindus?

Manu

Manu was a legendary holy man who lived in the distant past. His story can be found in the Matsya (Fish) Purana. At the time of Manu, humans had become evil, so Vishnu descended to earth as a small fish. In the story, the fish asks Manu to save it from the larger fish in its small pond. Manu shows compassion and cares for the fish himself, even though it grows so large that it needs to be housed in a river, and then outgrows even that.

Kind and caring as ever, Manu carries the fish to the ocean. As he does so, the fish reveals itself as Vishnu and declares that a great flood is going to wipe out humanity because of all the evil in the world. The fish tells Manu to build a ship that will save him and his family. Manu does this and Vishnu, still in the form of a giant fish, tows the ship through the raging waters.

When the flood is over, Manu's sacrifices to Vishnu enable him to repopulate the world. Hindus believe that Manu's devotion to God, and his compassion for his fellow creatures, are what saved humanity from extinction. He is still seen as an example to Hindus today.

The Matsya avatar of Vishnu tows Manu's boat to safety.

Shankara (CE 788–820)

Shankara lived in India around 1300 years ago. He became an ascetic when he was a teenager and went begging from door to door. One day, he knocked on the door of an old woman. Although she was poor, she did not want to send a holy man away with nothing, so she gave him her last piece of fruit. When Shankara realised how poor the woman was, he composed a hymn to Lakshmi, the goddess of wealth. The poor woman's devotion and Shankara's hymn delighted the goddess and the woman was rewarded with a shower of golden fruit.

Shankara's disciples learning from their guru.

Later in Shankara's life, he travelled around India and became renowned for his intelligence. He set up several monasteries and schools of Hindu philosophy. Shankara's love of learning and his humble devotion to God remain a powerful inspiration to many Hindus today.

Caitanya (1486–1534)

Like Shankara, Caitanya was very successful in his studies. He became a teacher at the age of 16 and was very proud of his academic achievements. However, his life changed after meeting a guru in northern India. Caitanya became devoted to Krishna, a form of Vishnu, and changed the way he lived. He was no longer puffed up with pride at his academic studies. Instead, he became convinced that the best way to live was to worship Krishna constantly. Caitanya worshipped by dancing, singing loudly, and laughing and jumping with joy at the thought of Krishna. Caitanya would be in **ecstasy** when he meditated on Krishna's loving, playful character.

Caitanya and disciples dancing. Note the contrast with Shankara and his disciples!

As Caitanya's style of worshipping Vishnu became popular, some more traditional Hindus complained to the local ruler, who was a Muslim, that Caitanya was causing trouble. According to legend, Caitanya and his followers responded to this by peacefully marching to the ruler's palace to speak to him. At Caitanya's kind, loving words, the ruler wept. He then joined Caitanya's followers in a song accompanied by a devotional dance.

Caitanya believed that bhakti was the best way to live, and his teaching and life inspired many Hindus. Even today, his emotional and ecstatic style of worship is followed in some Hindu communities, and he is a particularly revered saint among Vaishnavas.

Mata Amritanandamayi Devi (b. 1953)

Mata Devi, also known as Amma ('mother'), has become famous around the world as a great Hindu spiritual leader. From a young age, she was inspired to embrace people who appeared to be sad or in need of comfort. She resisted her parents' attempts to arrange a marriage for her because she wanted to serve humanity with all her strength. Her unconditional love and service to others inspired many Hindus to become her disciples. People began to travel from all parts of the world to receive a hug from her. Even non-Hindus who receive her hug and blessing describe it as an extraordinarily warm and moving experience.

Amma giving a hug to a follower. The man might have had to queue for hours to meet her.

Amma is now a revered guru and her charity donates millions of pounds a year to causes like disaster relief. Amma also promotes tolerance of different faiths.

> ### Key vocabulary
>
> **ecstasy** An extreme feeling of happiness and joy

Check your understanding

1. Why do Hindus see Manu as a good person?
2. Describe what happened when Shankara visited the old woman.
3. Describe the way that Caitanya worshipped Vishnu.
4. Explain the differences between Shankara and Caitanya.
5. Why might Hindus see Amma as an important spiritual teacher?

Unit 1: History and belief
Knowledge organiser

Key vocabulary

ascetic Someone who lives a simple life away from society, usually to become closer to the supreme being or to achieve moksha (also known as a sadhu)

Aum A sacred syllable or sound that is very important to Hindus and which they chant

avatar A god who descends to earth as a human or other animal in order to fight evil and re-establish goodness

bhakti A Sanskrit word meaning 'devotion' or 'worship'; some Hindus believe that bhakti alone can be a way to achieve moksha

Brahman A supreme being in which most modern Hindus believe; the source of everything, including the gods

chakra A word meaning 'wheel', one of the weapons that Hindu gods may carry

deity A god or goddess

dharma The moral law that Hindus must follow; the word can be translated as 'duty' or 'righteousness'

ecstasy An extreme feeling of happiness and joy

karma The forces that influence people's fortune and future reincarnation

Mahabharata An epic story that is inspirational for Hindus

meditation The practice of focusing the mind

moksha Escaping from samsara and never dying or becoming reincarnated again; the term literally means 'release'

monotheist Someone who believes in only one god

polytheistic Referring to belief in many gods; someone who believes in many gods is a polytheist

Purana A Hindu text that is more recent than the Vedas, but is still thought to contain profound wisdom and teachings

Ramayana An epic story that is inspirational for Hindus

reincarnated When a soul is reborn by passing into a new body

Rishis The Vedic people who first heard the Vedas and taught them to others

sacrifice A method of worship that involves offering animals or food to the gods

samsara The continual process of death and reincarnation; also, the entire universe as we know it

sanatana dharma Eternal dharma or law; this never changes and is always good, regardless of the time and place

Sanskrit A language used in ancient India, which many Hindu texts are written in

Shaiva A Hindu who believes that Shiva is the Supreme God

shruti A word referring to religious teachings that are revealed to Rishis directly from God

symbol An image that expresses religious ideas

tapas Literally 'heat'; ascetics and people practising yoga intensively generate tapas

Trimurti A term for the three main Hindu gods Brahma, Vishnu and Shiva

trishula A word meaning 'three spears', another weapon symbolising the power and authority of the gods

upanayana A traditional Hindu ceremony that children undergo when they are ready to be educated about the Vedas and other sacred texts

vahana An animal 'vehicle' that transports Hindu deities

Vaishnava A Hindu who believes that Vishnu is the Supreme God

Vedas A collection of sacred writings, literally meaning 'knowledge'

vibhuti The three white lines on Shiva's forehead, which represent his superhuman powers

yoga Controlling the mind and body to purify yourself and achieve moksha

Key facts

- The roots of Hinduism can be traced back to India more than 4000 years ago. Today, it has nearly one billion followers worldwide.

- Hinduism has no single founder and no particular leader or group of leaders. Its followers, known as Hindus, have many different beliefs.

- The main sacred texts in Hinduism are the four Vedas, which are believed to have been revealed by God.

- Other important texts for Hindus include the Mahabharata, the Ramayana and the Puranas, all of which contain stories about the gods and goddesses.

- Vaishnavas believe that Vishnu is the Supreme God; Shaivas believe that Shiva is the Supreme God. Local gods are often believed to be forms or extensions of the Supreme God.

- Hinduism is rich in symbolism. Objects such as the chakra (wheel), conch shell and lotus flower all have special meanings for Hindus.

- Hindus believe in reincarnation. What determines a person's next life is karma: whether a person performs good or bad deeds in this life.

- The journey of the soul through these reincarnations is called samsara. Hindus try to achieve a permanent release from samsara known as moksha. Moksha might be achieved through yoga and meditation or through worship and devotion.

- 'Dharma' is a universal law, meaning 'duty' or 'righteousness', which guides how Hindus live their lives. They try to show loyalty and respect and support charities to help those in need.

- Yoga and meditation are ways of controlling the body and mind to help achieve moksha. They involve moving the body in certain postures (asana), controlling breathing (pranayama) and focusing the mind so it is free of distractions.

- Ascetics are Hindus who choose to give up everyday comforts and live lives of hardship, often as beggars, to purify themselves and help them towards moksha.

Key people and gods

Agni The Vedic god of fire who consumed the food offered in sacrifices and made it acceptable to other gods

Arjuna A heroic character in the Mahabharata who obeys Krishna by fighting against his own family in order to follow dharma

Brahma One of the main three Hindu gods; the creator of the world

Brahman A supreme being in which most modern Hindus believe; the source of everything, including the gods

Caitanya An exuberant worshipper of Krishna who lived from 1486 to 1534

Ganesha The elephant-headed god of wisdom

Indra The Vedic god of sky, who sent thunderbolts to earth

Kalki A warrior on a white horse; the form that Hindus believe the final avatar of Vishnu will take

Krishna One of the avatars of Vishnu; a charioteer who instructs Arjuna how to live a good life. He is a very popular deity

Lakshmi The god Vishnu's wife; the goddess of wealth

Manu A legendary man saved by the fish avatar of Vishnu

Mata Devi (Amma) A modern Hindu teacher who people travel to receive a hug from

Parvati The god Shiva's wife; a goddess of love and fertility

Rama King in the Ramayana whose wife Sita is abducted by Ravana; he defeats Ravana

Ravana The many-armed demon who abducted Sita

Rudra A much-feared Vedic god who inflicted illness upon farm animals

Shankara An intelligent ascetic who lived 1300 years ago

Shiva One of the main three Hindu gods; the destroyer of the world

Sita The wife of Rama in the Ramayana kidnapped by Ravana

Vishnu One of the main three Hindu gods; the preserver of the world

Vishvamitra A character in the Ramayana who had built up massive power and great abilities by meditating and fasting

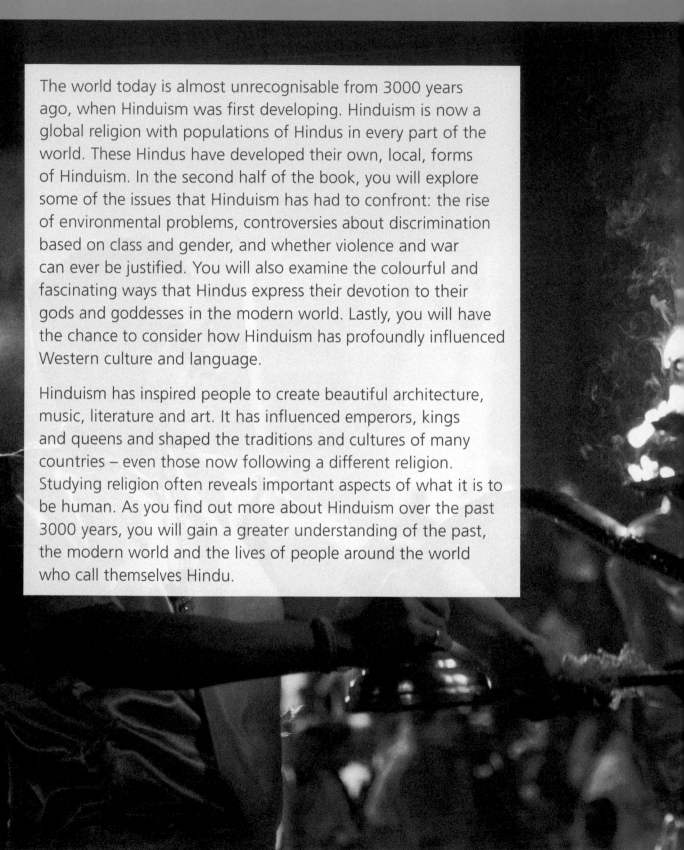

Hinduism in the modern world

The world today is almost unrecognisable from 3000 years ago, when Hinduism was first developing. Hinduism is now a global religion with populations of Hindus in every part of the world. These Hindus have developed their own, local, forms of Hinduism. In the second half of the book, you will explore some of the issues that Hinduism has had to confront: the rise of environmental problems, controversies about discrimination based on class and gender, and whether violence and war can ever be justified. You will also examine the colourful and fascinating ways that Hindus express their devotion to their gods and goddesses in the modern world. Lastly, you will have the chance to consider how Hinduism has profoundly influenced Western culture and language.

Hinduism has inspired people to create beautiful architecture, music, literature and art. It has influenced emperors, kings and queens and shaped the traditions and cultures of many countries – even those now following a different religion. Studying religion often reveals important aspects of what it is to be human. As you find out more about Hinduism over the past 3000 years, you will gain a greater understanding of the past, the modern world and the lives of people around the world who call themselves Hindu.

2.1	Forms and places of worship	28
2.2	Places of pilgrimage	30
2.3	Hindu festivals	32
2.4	What is the caste system?	34
2.5	Hindu attitudes to violence	36
2.6	Do Hindus believe in gender equality?	38
2.7	What are Hindu attitudes to the environment?	40
2.8	Hinduism in world culture	42
Knowledge organiser		44

Forms and places of worship

How do Hindus express their devotion in worship?

Puja

In Vedic times, Hindu worship often involved public sacrifices of animals or food. Today, these only happen in a small number of Hindu communities. Most Hindu homes have a shrine in them and Hindus perform **puja**, or worship, at home. These shrines usually contain an image of the deity or deities that are most important to that particular family. Offerings of flowers, fruit and coconuts are placed in front of the images. These offerings keep alive the tradition of Hindu sacrifice that goes back over 3000 years. Hindus often also recite **mantras** at home every day.

66 This is the Gayatri Mantra, a very famous mantra that some Hindus chant in the morning at sunrise.

om bhur bhuvaḥ svaḥ
tát savitúr váreṇyaṃ
bhárgo devásya dhımahī
dhíyo yó naḥ prachodayat

('We meditate on the supremely radiant glory of the divine Light; may he inspire our understanding.') 99
Rig Veda 3.62.10[11] (translated by S. Radhakrishnan)

A shrine in a Hindu home.

Murti and darshan

The image of a deity found at a Hindu shrine or temple is called a **murti**, which means 'form' or 'image'. Whether in a temple or a home, the murti is a sacred object. A murti is not a deity itself – it is just an image of the deity. However, Hindus believe that if it is produced and installed in the right way then the murti has a special connection to the deity.

The word **darshan** is used to describe a special way of seeing a murti. In darshan, a Hindu focuses on the murti in a particular, devoted way, making this 'seeing' an act of worship. Hindus believe that by seeing the murti in this way, they will receive blessings and a sort of energy or force from the deity. In temples, murtis are usually hidden behind a curtain most of the time, but if people go to the temple at the right time darshan will be given. This means that the murti will be briefly revealed so that people can express their devotion to the deity.

This murti is in a temple to Venkateshwara, a form of Vishnu, in India. The priests treat it with great reverence.

Sometimes, darshan can also be of a holy man or woman. Hindus might travel to receive darshan from a holy person. Seeing such a person provides an opportunity to express devotion to the deity to which the holy man or woman has dedicated their life. Hindus believe that it is important to be clean and well-presented when receiving darshan, so they often wash beforehand. Hindus believe that if they are standing in the presence of a murti, they are, in a way, standing in the presence of God, so this is definitely a time to dress up!

Mandirs

Some Hindus worship regularly at a temple while others might just visit during festivals or on other special occasions. Some Hindu temples in Asia are more than 1500 years old, but there are many more modern temples. Hindu temples are sometimes called **mandirs**. Much thought goes into building mandirs. For example, they are sometimes planned on a grid of 64 squares, which is considered a particularly sacred number. This is because it is the square of eight, and some deities are considered to have eight powers or eight forms.

In many temples, the space in the very centre is the most sacred part, and is often where the murti is kept. All the other features of the temple, such as statues and altars, are arranged around the centre. This is seen as mirroring the universe, because the whole universe, including demons, humans, gods, heavens and hells, revolve around the Supreme Deity.

Sometimes Hindus bring special offerings such as colourful flowers to the temple to offer as puja to their chosen deity.

Akshardham Temple, New Delhi. The different levels of the building represent the different levels of the universe, with God at the top.

Key vocabulary

darshan 'Seeing' God; a form of worship and devotion in which the murti of a deity is revealed to worshippers

mandir A Hindu term for a temple

mantra An extract from a sacred text that is chanted repeatedly during worship

murti An image of a god or goddess

puja The Sanskrit word for worship

Check your understanding

1 What is puja?
2 What religious activities do Hindus perform in the home?
3 What is a murti?
4 Why is darshan important for Hindus?
5 Explain how Hindu temples or mandirs are built in a symbolic way.

Places of pilgrimage

Pilgrimages are long and difficult journeys. Why do Hindus undertake them?

Pilgrimage is important to Hindus, and they make journeys to many different places for worship. Pilgrimage sites are known as **tirtha**, which means 'crossing place'. This is because a tirtha is a place where gods or goddesses are believed to come to earth to defeat evil or to become part of the world.

Varanasi

For many Hindus, the city of Varanasi in India, which has more than 200 temples, is an important pilgrimage destination. It lies on the banks of the river Ganges (Ganga in Sanskrit), which has been sacred to Hindus for thousands of years. Ganga is worshipped as a goddess. In Hindu myths, Brahma ordered Ganga to descend to earth so that the many sons of a great king could achieve moksha. Ganga was annoyed at this request and hurled herself to earth with the intention of washing it away. Shiva caught Ganga in his matted hair (see the picture on page 11) and this saved all life on earth. As Ganga trickled through the locks of Shiva's hair, she landed softly, forming the river Ganges. Hindus believe that bathing in the Ganges removes bad karma from past acts.

Hindus also believe that Varanasi is one of the best places on earth for their ashes to be scattered after they pass away. Having your ashes scattered in the Ganges is believed to be beneficial for your next reincarnation and brings you closer to achieving moksha. In Varanasi there are many locations along the river where devout Hindus' bodies can be cremated on a traditional funeral pyre and scattered in the sacred waters of the river.

Puri

The ancient city of Puri is the centre of devotion to a form of Vishnu known as Jagannath. Pilgrims have visited the city for centuries, and today millions of Hindus make the journey every year. One of the many attractions in Puri is the temple of Jagannath, built over 800 years ago. The temple has two large chakras on its towers, which represent the unimaginably powerful weapon that Vishnu wields. Darshan is given every day in the temple, when people are allowed to see the jewelled throne on which the murtis of the deities sit. There are over 100 shrines in the temple, so pilgrims can also show their devotion by walking around the temple and performing puja at one of these.

> **Fact**
>
> Enduring the difficulty of a journey for religious reasons is something that builds up good karma. For this reason, pilgrimage is as much about the journey as the destination.

The smoke in this picture is from a funeral pyre on the edge of the sacred river Ganges, in Varanasi.

The Temple of Jagannath.

The Kumbh Mela

The **Kumbh Mela** is one of the largest gatherings anywhere in the world. It is a festival that takes place every three years. The location of the Kumbh Mela alternates between four different venues in India so that each location hosts the festival once every twelve years. Up to 30 million pilgrims can descend on the Kumbh Mela in a single day! During this pilgrimage, people bathe in the sacred rivers of India, including the Ganges, in order to get rid of bad karma.

A procession of sadhus at the Kumbh Mela in 2013, at Allahabad.

The Kumbh Mela is also famous for attracting many ascetics, or sadhus, who often make the pilgrimage in large groups. For ordinary Hindus, the chance to see these sadhus is an important reason to make a Kumbh Mela pilgrimage. The sight of a holy man or woman is darshan; it is considered a blessing to have the chance to see such people, and many Hindus make offerings to them or ask for spiritual advice. Putting up with the heat and crowded conditions at the Kumbh Mela in order to bathe in the Ganges and see the sadhus is what pilgrimage is about for many Hindus.

Activity

Create a brochure that provides Hindus with information about popular pilgrimage sites.

Key vocabulary

Kumbh Mela Hindu festival when ascetics bathe in a river to remove karma; it takes place every three years

tirtha A 'crossing place' where a deity enters the human world; for this reason, they are places of pilgrimage

Fact

In the Mahabharata epic, which is over 2000 years old, Arjuna goes on a pilgrimage to the river Ganges. By visiting tirthas, Hindus are continuing a tradition contained in some of the most ancient stories in the world.

Check your understanding

1. What does the word 'tirtha' mean?
2. Why do many Hindus believe that the river Ganges is sacred?
3. What do Hindus believe about Varanasi?
4. Explain why Hindus would want to see a sadhu.
5. 'The journey is the most important part of Hindu pilgrimage.' Discuss this statement.

Unit 2: Hinduism in the modern world
Hindu festivals

What are the meanings of Hindu festivals?

Hundreds of Hindu festivals are celebrated around the world. They allow Hindus to step out of ordinary life and celebrate their religion and its traditions. However, because Hinduism has developed differently in different parts of the world, Hindus do not all celebrate the same festivals.

Diwali

Diwali is a five-day festival celebrated by almost all Hindus. The timing of Diwali is based on the Hindu lunar calendar. This means that it takes place at a different time each year in the UK, but it normally falls near the end of October or the start of November. During Diwali, Hindus light many lamps and candles, so it is sometimes called the 'festival of lights'.

Diwali decorations in Leicester, UK.

Today, Diwali has different meanings for different Hindus. For some, the glow of lights at Diwali symbolises the sun's nourishing energy, and is a reminder to Hindus of their dependence on the Supreme Deity who created this world, sustains it and will eventually destroy it. Another reason why some Hindus light lamps at Diwali is to help Lakshmi, the goddess of wealth, enter their homes and bring them good fortune.

Other Hindus remember the events of the Ramayana at Diwali. For them, the lights are a reminder of Rama and Sita returning home after defeating the demon Ravana (see page 14). They arrived at Ayodhya on a moonless night. In order to guide the couple home and welcome them, the people of the city lit lamps. For many Hindus, therefore, Diwali is partly about celebrating the victory of good over evil.

Some see Diwali as a reminder of a legend from the Vedas about a good Brahmin boy called Nachiketas who meets Yama, the god of death. Yama offers to grant the boy three wishes. For his first two wishes, Nachiketas asks for peace for his family and to know more about sacrifice. For his third wish, he asks to know what happens after death. Yama is reluctant to answer this and urges Nachiketas to ask for wealth or long life. However, Nachiketas insists on an answer to his question. Yama praises Nachiketas for making a truly wise choice and explains Hindu beliefs about the soul and reincarnation to him. The lights at Diwali are thought to symbolise knowledge and wisdom defeating ignorance and darkness.

Thaipusam

Although many Hindus worship Vishnu or Shiva as the Supreme Deity, these gods take different forms. In the festival of **Thaipusam**, Shaivas worship a form of Shiva called Murugan – a fierce god of war. The festival is particularly celebrated in southern India, Malaysia, Singapore and Sri Lanka. Some devout Hindus express their devotion to Murugan by fasting for several weeks before the festival.

During Thaipusam, there are large, colourful processions of worshippers and murtis of Murugan. Some Hindus take on a **kavadi**, or 'burden', during the festival. This might mean carrying something heavy during the long Thaipusam procession to the temple. Other devotees have their faces and bodies pierced with spikes as a kavadi; others carry a huge shrine on their backs. The idea behind fasting and taking on such burdens is to show devotion to God and a willingness to sacrifice comfort and fine living for him.

The Ratha Yatra

The city of Puri is a popular pilgrimage site, but it also hosts a festival called the **Ratha Yatra**. 'Ratha' means 'chariot' in Sanskrit. In ancient India chariots were important in warfare and were symbols of power because warriors rode into battle in them. During the Ratha Yatra, murtis of Jagannath and other deities of the temple are placed in chariots and pulled through the city. Families spend months building the chariots from local wood in a very precise way in order to show their devotion to Jagannath.

A kavadi bearer in Singapore during Thaipusam.

Jagannath's 16-wheeled chariot at Ratha Yatra.

The murtis are visible for all to see during the procession, so the Ratha Yatra festival gives an opportunity for darshan. This is especially important for those unable to make it into the Jagannath temple to receive darshan there.

Key vocabulary

Diwali The festival of lights, celebrated by nearly all Hindus

kavadi A burden carried during the Thaipusam festival to express devotion to Murugan

Ratha Yatra A Vaishnava festival in Puri, involving a procession of murtis in chariots

Thaipusam A Shaiva festival to worship Murugan, the god of war

Check your understanding

1. What is Diwali often called and how long does it last?
2. Explain in detail two ways in which Diwali reminds Hindus of their beliefs and legends.
3. Explain what devotees do at Thaipusam and why.
4. Why is the Ratha Yatra important to Vaishnavas?
5. Why are there so many different Hindu festivals and why are they celebrated differently?

Unit 2: Hinduism in the modern world
What is the caste system?

How have Hindu beliefs about caste changed?

According to some ancient Hindu texts, every person belonged to one of four classes, or castes. The caste that a person belonged to determined the job that he or she did. The system was intended to create a balanced community in which everyone did an important job that was required for society to function well. This way of organising society is known as the **caste system**.

From the earliest times, people viewed some castes as higher or lower than others. They also tended to believe that people were born into a caste with the qualities needed to perform a role (which meant that a person could not move between castes). They thought that following dharma meant fulfilling the duty of the person's caste. These ideas were supported by an ancient Hindu text called the Laws of Manu. The four castes, in order of how highly they were viewed, were:

These dalit women in India are using a bank designed to help rural people lift themselves out of poverty.

Brahmins: priests who looked after spiritual matters
Kshatriyas: warriors who protected society
Vaishyas: traders and farmers
Shudras: manual labourers/servants

The myth of Purusha

There is a myth about the caste system in the Rig Veda. In it, a giant called Purusha is sacrificed by the gods in order to create human society. Each caste is made from a different part of Purusha's body. The Brahmins were made from Purusha's head, showing they are thoughtful and spiritual. The Kshatriyas were made from Purusha's arms, meaning they should be strong and ready to fight against injustice. The Vaishyas were made from Purusha's thighs and the Shudras were made from his feet. Because feet are often seen as unpleasant, this could suggest that Shudras are of lower status. However, feet are also a vital part of the body, holding everything else up. As such, Hindus can interpret this myth as showing that each class is a vital and valued part of society and no caste is more important than another.

Fact

In ancient times, some Hindus even believed that Untouchables should ring a bell when they entered a village so that people could hide. This is not widely believed today.

The Untouchables

As people started to view castes as higher or lower, a fifth group developed. Members of this group were known as 'Untouchables', and no other caste would associate with them. We do not know exactly where this group came from or who became part of it, but we do know that they were regarded as lower than the Shudras. They were considered impure and had to do the most menial jobs. Unable to move caste, Untouchables faced a life of poverty and discrimination.

Activity

Prepare a case arguing either for or against the statement 'The caste system is a good thing.' Then hold a class debate.

Gandhi and the Dalits

Mohandas Gandhi is probably the most famous Hindu of the twentieth century. Gandhi taught that all Hindus are equal in God's eyes. He believed that Untouchables should be treated like any other Hindus, calling them 'Harijans', which means 'children of God'. Gandhi worked hard to end the discrimination Untouchables faced. For example, he campaigned for them to be allowed to worship inside temples, which many people were angry about. He also caused great controversy by accepting an Untouchable family a community or settlement he had developed and adopting their daughter.

The modern Indian name given to Untouchables is Dalits, which means 'oppressed' or 'broken'. Dalits prefer this term because it acknowledges that they are not really 'untouchable' and have been (and still are) oppressed. In India today, approximately 15 per cent of the population are Dalits. They still face problems in many places, and people continue to campaign to rid society of caste-based discrimination.

Gandhi speaking to Dalit workers in 1940.

The caste system today

Most modern Hindus do not think that following dharma requires people to do a specific job that they were born to do. Like Gandhi, many Hindus also believe that all human beings are of equal worth. Since 1950, laws have been passed in India to try to protect and support the lower castes. For example, there are a certain number of places reserved for non-Brahmins in schools and colleges, also for Dalits in government. Caste has not entirely disappeared in modern Indian society. Many people continue to remember their ancestral 'jati', or trade, which is a type of caste system. In some parts of rural India the caste system is also still important. Even outside India, many people still choose to marry within their own caste.

This man is a journalist from a dalit community in a slum area of Mumbai. He is showing his son a news report he produced to highlight the discrimination that dalits still face.

Key vocabulary

Caste System A series of social classes that determine someone's job and status in society

Check your understanding

1. What do Hindus think was the original intention of the caste system?
2. Explain two ways in which the myth of Purusha in the Rig Veda could be interpreted.
3. How can ideas about caste cause discrimination?
4. Explain how 'Untouchables' were treated and why they prefer the name 'Dalits'.
5. How effective have modern Hindus been at challenging caste-based discrimination? Refer to the actions of Gandhi in your answer.

Hindu attitudes to violence

What do Hindus believe about violence?

Violence in the Vedas

It is often said that religion is a source of conflict. Some people even say that if there were no religion there would be far less conflict in the world. There are parts of the Vedas that can be seen as celebrating violence. Vedic Hindus probably feared attack from neighbouring tribes, and this is reflected in their hymns. For example, in the Rig Veda there is a hymn to the weapons of war.

However, it also says in the Vedas: 'May all beings look at me with a friendly eye, may I do likewise, and may we look at each other with the eyes of a friend.' This shows that from early in the development of their faith, Hindus believed that harming other creatures should be avoided where possible. Some Hindus go further than this, and believe in **pantheism** – the idea that God is not only everywhere, but in everything too. As such, harming any living thing should be avoided because it is harming God. Because of these beliefs, many Hindus choose to be vegetarian, and the majority of Hindus no longer sacrifice animals to gods.

Arjuna in the Mahabharata

Hindus believe that sometimes dharma requires a person to fight. Arjuna, a legendary hero, questions Krishna about this in the Bhagavad Gita. At first, Arjuna believes that it is wrong for him to fight because it will involve killing and destruction on a large scale and he will have to fight against his own family. Krishna convinces him otherwise. Arjuna is a member of the Kshatriya (warrior) caste, and the battle is part of a war that is just. Therefore, it is his dharma to fight in the battle, despite his concerns about it. However, Krishna does say that Arjuna should perform his duty in a calm and detached manner. He shouldn't fight in the battle because he takes pleasure in fighting or killing. Rather, he should only fight because it is his duty. As such, the Bhagavad Gita says to fight only when it is absolutely necessary. It does not glorify fighting or killing.

A scene from the Bhagavad Gita showing Arjuna in battle.

Gandhi and non-violence

There is an ancient idea in Hinduism called **ahimsa**, which literally means 'non-injury' or 'no harm'. This means that Hindus try to resolve conflict peacefully and show kindness to other creatures. One of the most famous modern examples of ahimsa comes from Gandhi. In the first part of the twentieth century, India was part of the British Empire, but Gandhi believed it should be a country in its own right, so he began a long but peaceful campaign to win independence for India. Even when his followers were arrested or attacked by their opponents, they would not retaliate, hurl insults or show any other aggression. Instead, they refused to follow instructions from the authorities, went on strike and fasted. Through peaceful methods, they tried to persuade the Indian population and the British authorities that it was time for India to be independent. Eventually, they succeeded.

Gandhi believed that it is better to convince people of the truth of your ideas than to force ideas on an opponent using violence. He felt that following ahimsa allowed the justice, truth and goodness of his campaign to be clearly seen by the authorities. By using ancient Hindu ideas about ahimsa, Gandhi achieved a modern political goal. Many Hindus greatly respect him for this reason and he is often called 'Mahatma' Gandhi, which means 'great soul'.

> 66 Non violence… is a weapon for the brave. 99
> Mohandas Gandhi

Fact

Ahimsa is also part of yoga. Yogins seek to control emotions like anger, hatred and aggression because no one can reach moksha if unable to control these things. As such, yogins try to be peaceful and perfectly calm. They see violent people as being unable to control themselves, and therefore a long way from moksha.

Key vocabulary

ahimsa Literally 'non-harming' or 'non-violence'; a Hindu teaching that encourages peaceful resolution of conflict and kindness towards other living creatures

pantheism The belief that God is in everything

Mahatma Gandhi under arrest. He refused to resist arrest or to allow his followers to use violence to rescue him.

Check your understanding

1. Describe Vedic ideas about violence.
2. What is pantheism?
3. What advice does Krishna give Arjuna in the Bhagavad Gita?
4. Explain how Gandhi put the idea of ahimsa into practice.
5. Why is ahimsa important to yogins?

Unit 2: Hinduism in the modern world
Do Hindus believe in gender equality?

Do Hindu women have a different role from men?

Vedic India

Ancient India was a **patriarchal society**, and men and women had very different roles. Typically, men were leaders, while women were expected to become experts at looking after their homes. Women were not allowed to become priests or perform sacrifices to the gods, but there were some religious duties that they were responsible for. For example, a wife was required to keep a fire continually burning at the shrine in her home.

Even today, there are very few female priests and temple leaders, and some Hindu temples in India only permit men to enter. However, in the twenty-first century, Hindus are beginning to re-examine the roles of men and women. Some modern Hindus believe that everyone should be free to choose a role and a place within society that is right for them, regardless of their gender. For example, in the past, it was mainly men who became ascetics, but now there are also female ascetics who practise yoga and other religious activities full time. These ascetics often live with others who have dedicated themselves to a spiritual life.

A female ascetic in Varanasi, Uttar Pradesh, India.

Sati

Traditionally, when Hindus die, they are cremated on an open funeral fire called a pyre. One reason for this is that Hindus believe the body is no longer significant once the soul has departed, so there is no need to preserve it. A few ancient Hindu writings mention a controversial custom called **sati**. This is when a woman whose husband has passed away throws herself on his funeral pyre so she can be with him immediately in the next life.

The Vedas and other respected sources do not mention sati and it was probably never a common practice. However, it may have happened occasionally in the history of Hinduism. In the past, Hindu widows were expected to remain single for the rest of their lives. Today, Hindus increasingly accept remarriage, and many women feel that they are able to remarry if their husband has died.

> 66 We should not think that we are men and women, but only that we are human beings, born to cherish and to help one another. 99
> Swami Vivekananda (1863–1902), a modern Hindu teacher

Ancient texts

The Laws of Manu, an ancient collection of Hindu teachings written more than 2000 years ago, is a controversial text, and some Hindus think that its teachings about women are unsuitable for the modern world. For example, the Laws of Manu state that a woman should be protected in childhood by her father, in adulthood by her husband and in old age by her sons. Some Hindus think that this shows respect to women by encouraging men to protect them. However, others think that the teaching stops women living independent lives.

The oldest Hindu texts are called the Vedas. It is difficult to know exactly who composed the Vedas because they were written down more than 2500 years ago, but it is likely that most of them were composed by men. However, in the oldest of the four Vedas, the Rig Veda, some hymns and poems are written by people who have what seem to be female names. Some modern Hindus see this as evidence that even in Vedic times women were viewed as wise and were respected in religious matters. There are also Hindu texts that mention women who were excellent at yoga, meditation and teaching. Therefore, some Hindus argue that women should have an important role in religious matters today. They say that dharma depends on the individual, not on gender.

Fact

Hindu women often have a coloured dot on the middle of their forehead. This is called a bindi. In the past, the bindi was a way that women showed that they were happily married. Nowadays, it is sometimes a way of showing wellbeing, or it can be a way of marking the 'third eye', which is viewed as one of the body's energy points.

Key vocabulary

patriarchal society A culture that is dominated or controlled by men

sati When a woman throws herself on to her husband's funeral pyre

Check your understanding

1. How was society patriarchal in Vedic times?
2. How are attitudes towards gender changing in Hinduism?
3. What is sati? Explain Hindu views on it.
4. Why are the Laws of Manu controversial?
5. 'Men and women should have different roles in society.' Discuss this statement with reference to Hinduism.

What are Hindu attitudes to the environment?

Can ancient teachings show Hindus how to respond to environmental problems?

Earth as a goddess

In Hindu writings, the earth is often referred to as a goddess called **Bhumi Devi** or 'Mother Earth'. Mother Earth is bountiful and provides humans with everything they need. Another way of referring to the earth is **dharti**, meaning 'she who holds everything'. Hindus believe that the earth is sacred and should be treated with respect, care and love. Causing damage to the environment is an act of disrespect to Bhumi Devi, while repairing and improving the environment shows great love and respect for her.

The battle for the heavens

At the start of the Mahabharata, there is a story about a battle between the gods and the demons over who should get to live in the heavens. The demons lost, so began to be born on earth. So many demons were born that the earth could not support all the creatures on it, as swarms of them exploited its natural resources and the animals that lived there.

Eventually, Bhumi Devi went to the god Brahma, the creator of the world, to ask for help. Brahma told the other gods to descend to earth to destroy the demons, restoring harmony and balance to Bhumi Devi. Some Hindus see this story as a very old example of taking care of our planet and a warning against taking the earth's resources for granted.

Wall mural of Goddess of Earth, Bhumi Devi.

> 66 Mother Bhumi, may whatever I dig from you grow back again quickly, and may we not injure you by our labour. 99
>
> Atharvaveda

> ### Fact
>
> Many Hindus view cows as particularly sacred creatures, and slaughtering or eating them is illegal in many parts of India. Cows are sometimes seen as a symbol of the earth and representative of all other creatures.

The Chipko movement

The Chipko movement has inspired many Hindus to take an interest in the environment. This began in the 1960s when women in a rural part of India called Gopeshwar became concerned that forests in the area were being chopped down. For hundreds of years, local people had depended on the forests for survival, and they believed the trees were sacred. They saw it as their duty to preserve them for future generations and to maintain a balance in the local environment, so they decided to protest.

Women in the Chipko movement hugged trees for days – sometimes weeks – to stop them being cut down. These women gained the support of other villagers and successfully, but peacefully, confronted armed police, violent woodcutters and local politicians to prevent their forests being destroyed. Eventually, the prime minister of India was convinced to ban the cutting down of trees in certain areas.

Green Pilgrimage Network

A pilgrimage is a journey to a holy place. People often return from pilgrimages refreshed and more committed to their religion. Pilgrimages have been popular among Hindus for 2000 years, but in the last century more Hindus than ever have travelled to holy sites in India. One popular site is the city of Puri with its temple to Jagannath. It was built over 800 years ago and attracts millions of pilgrims every year. When thousands or millions of people make the same pilgrimage in a short space of time, the environmental impact can be huge. Places like Puri suffer from litter, lack of water, air pollution from vehicles and many other problems.

Women of the Chipko movement protecting a tree.

Some Hindus are keen to make sure that pilgrimages have as little impact on the environment as possible. In recent years, Hindus have set up the Green Pilgrimage Network. They try to reduce the number of vehicles around temples in Puri. They also clean up gardens and areas of natural beauty and develop green energy sources for temples and pilgrimage sites. They do this because they believe that devotion to gods or goddesses should not come at the expense of Bhumi Devi.

Activity

Design a leaflet that raises awareness among Hindus of the importance of looking after the environment. Your leaflet should:

- explain why Hindus should care about the environment
- describe an example of inspirational work
- explain what Hindus can do or are doing to help the environment.

Millions of pilgrims visit Puri every year for religious festivals. The environmental impact can be significant.

Key vocabulary

Bhumi Devi 'Mother Earth' – earth seen as a goddess

dharti 'She who holds everything' – a way of referring to the earth goddess

Check your understanding

1. Explain why Hindu beliefs about reincarnation might lead them to want to protect the environment.
2. Why do Hindus believe that the earth is special?
3. What happens in the story about demons at the start of the Mahabharata?
4. Describe how the Chipko movement helped to protect the environment.
5. 'Hindu beliefs help to protect the environment.' Discuss this statement.

Unit 2: Hinduism in the modern world
Hinduism in world culture

How have Hindu ideas influenced world culture?

Hinduism in Western culture

Some words in the English language have been part of Hinduism for a long time. For example, 'karma' is an idea found in Hindu culture for over 2500 years, but it is now fairly common to hear it used even by non-Hindus. 'Yoga' is similarly old. Yoga was once mainly practised by ascetics, with the aim of achieving moksha. Today, however, non-Hindus around the world practise yoga and meditation. Yoga has become a popular way for people of all religions to relax, get fit and stay healthy.

A genetically engineered avatar from the 2009 film Avatar.

The words 'mantra' and 'guru' are also sometimes used in English. A mantra is a sacred phrase repeated by Hindus. In English, it is used to describe a phrase or motto that someone lives by. In Sanskrit, 'guru' means a respected teacher. In English, 'guru' describes someone who is an expert on a certain subject. Look online and you will find management 'gurus' and marketing 'gurus'. Your teacher may even have met education 'gurus'!

Sometimes people use the word 'avatar' to mean a picture that is chosen to represent a player in a game or on social media on the internet. Film director James Cameron was inspired by the Hindu idea of an avatar when writing and directing his 2009 film Avatar. In the movie, a human's intelligence and consciousness is implanted into a genetically engineered alien body in order to communicate with aliens on a planet that humans cannot inhabit. Avatar is a science-fiction film about humans hundreds of years in the future, inspired by a very ancient idea.

The Mahabharata on screen

In India, the Mahabharata has inspired several film and television shows. It is difficult to tell the entire story of the Mahabharata, as it contains over 1.8 million words, but in 1988 an Indian television series called *Mahabharat* attempted to do this. It ran for 94 episodes over 2 years and was incredibly popular. For many Hindus, it was inspiring to see the eternal battle between good and evil recreated on television. The series was so successful that it was also shown in the UK.

The Mahabharata and Ramayana in puppets and dance

In ancient times, Hindu myths and stories were often performed on stage through song and dance. In Indonesia, a type of puppet theatre called Wayang developed. Traditional Wayang theatre is still performed in

Indonesia today. Beautiful puppets are used to perform traditional Hindu stories such as the Mahabharata or Ramayana. Often, the puppets are not directly seen – instead, they are used to create shadows on a piece of white cloth, with light provided by an oil lamp. The stories are narrated by a dalang, a performer skilled at using his or her voice to convey the drama and emotion of the epic stories. An orchestra provides musical accompaniment.

These puppets are in a traditional Wayang shadow puppet show of a story from the Mahabharata.

In Thailand, most people are Buddhists, not Hindus. However, there is a traditional form of theatre called Khon, which involves performing stories from the Thai version of the Ramayana, the Ramakien. Khon theatre is performed by dancers who often wear masks and elaborate, shining costumes. They practise for years to learn the graceful dance movements that express the story. The Ramakien gives a larger role to Hanuman and his army of monkeys than the Ramayana does, and their costumes on stage are particularly dramatic. The Mahabharata and Ramayana present such powerful stories of good triumphing over evil that they have proved popular around the world for over 2000 years.

The dancer in the centre is Hanuman in this Thai Khon theatre production of stories from the Ramayana.

Hinduism around the world

Hinduism has influenced the culture of the world for millennia. It has touched non-Hindu cultures and produced some of the world's greatest art, architecture and literature. Because Hinduism has such a rich culture, it is also highly diverse. If there is one lesson to take away from studying Hinduism, it is to realise how different it can be around the world. Its culture is wide, rich and fascinating.

Activity

Draw a table and list as many similarities and differences as you can between Hinduism and any other religion that you have studied.

Check your understanding

1 Give three examples of words that have entered English from Sanskrit and Hinduism.

2 Why has yoga become popular among non-Hindus?

3 Explain what an avatar is in Hinduism and in the 2009 film.

4 Describe how the Mahabharata and Ramayana are portrayed in Indonesia and Thailand.

5 Using ideas from this book, discuss why Hinduism might be said to be 'diverse'.

Unit 2: Hinduism in the modern world
Knowledge organiser

Key vocabulary

ahimsa Literally 'non-harming' or 'non-violence', a Hindu teaching that encourages peaceful resolution of conflict and kindness towards other living creatures

caste system A series of social classes that determine someone's job and status in society

darshan 'Seeing' God; a form of worship and devotion in which the murti of a deity is revealed to worshippers

dharti 'She who holds everything' – a way of referring to the earth goddess

Diwali The festival of lights, celebrated by nearly all Hindus

kavadi A burden carried during the Thaipusam festival to express devotion to Murugan

mandir A Hindu term for a temple

mantra An extract from a sacred text that is chanted repeatedly during worship

murti An image of a god or goddess

pantheism The belief that God is in everything

patriarchal society A culture that is dominated or controlled by men

puja The Sanskrit word for worship

Ratha Yatra A Vaishnava festival in Puri involving a procession of murtis in chariots

sati When a woman throws herself on to her husband's funeral pyre

Thaipusam A Shaiva festival to worship Murugan, the god of war

tirtha A 'crossing place', where a deity enters the human world; for this reason, tirthas are places of pilgrimage

Key facts

- Hindu worship is called puja, and it may be done at a shrine in the home or in a temple. The image of a deity in a shrine or temple is called a murti. Hindus 'see' or worship these in a special way called darshan.

- Making a pilgrimage to one of Hinduism's many holy sites is believed to create good karma. Key pilgrimage sites include Varanasi on the river Ganges and the city of Puri.

- Hindus in different parts of the world celebrate different festivals, but almost all Hindus celebrate Diwali, the festival of lights. It means different things to different people: Diwali may be to honour the Supreme Deity, or to remember the events of the Ramayana or a legend from the Vedas.

- The caste system is a social structure mentioned in some ancient Hindu texts. It divides society into four classes, which later developed into five, with the 'Untouchables', or Dalits, at the bottom. Mohandas Gandhi campaigned to stop discrimination against the Dalits, although they still face problems today.

- Hindus believe it is important to avoid harming other creatures, summed up in the ancient idea of ahisma, which means 'non-harming'.

- In ancient times, Hindu men and women had different roles in society. Although there is more gender equality today, there are still not many female Hindu priests or temple leaders.

- Hindus respect and value the earth because it provides people with everything they need to survive. For this reason, they work hard to protect it against environmental problems.

- Ancient Hindu ideas have influenced popular culture through the centuries, for example in the form of practices such as yoga and meditation, theatre shows and films.

Key people and gods

Bhumi Devi 'Mother Earth' – the earth seen as a goddess

Gandhi A Hindu who lived from 1869 to 1948 who opposed caste-based discrimination and led peaceful protests for Indian independence

Ganga A goddess who formed the river Ganges

Jagannath An important deity for many Hindus, believed to be a form of Vishnu

Murugan A fierce god of war, a form of Shiva, worshipped by Shaivas at Thaipusam

Purusha A mythical giant whose vast body was sacrificed by the gods to create human society

Yama The god of death

Murugan Golden Statue at Battuck caves, Kuala lampur, Malaysia, Asia.

Hindu priests in India worship goddess Durga during the Hindu festival of Dussera.

Index

Agni 9, 25
agnosticism 4
ahimsa (non-violence) 37, 44
altars, sacrificial 9
animal sacrifice 9, 28, 36
Arjuna 15, 19, 25, 31, 36
asanas 20
ascetics 20–1, 22, 24, 25, 31, 38, 42
Atharvaveda 40
atheism 4
Aum (Om) 12, 13, 24
avatars 11, 24, 42
    of Vishnu 10, 12, 15, 19, 22, 23, 25
Ayodhya 14, 32

Bhagavad Gita 15, 17, 19, 36
Bhagavad Purana 15
bhakti 17, 23, 24
Bhumi Devi (Mother Earth) 40, 41, 45
bindi 39
Brahma 10, 25, 30, 40
Brahman 11, 24, 25
Brahmins (priest caste) 34
breath control 20
Brihadaranyaka Upanishad 17
Buddha 10
Buddhism 4, 17, 43

Caitanya 23, 25
caste system 34–5, 44
chakras (wheels) 12, 13, 24, 30
charity 18
Chipko movement 40–1
compassion 22
conch shell, symbolism of 12
cows, sacred 40
creator 10, 11
cremation 38

dalangs 43
Dalits (Untouchables) 34–5
dance 23, 42–3
darshan 28–31, 29, 33, 44
death 6, 32, 38
deities 10–13, 11, 24, 28–9
    see also God; goddesses; gods; Supreme
        God; Supreme Goddess
demons 14, 15, 18, 29, 40
devotion 15, 17, 22–3, 28–9, 33
dharma 18–19, 24, 25, 35–6
dharti 40, 41, 44
dhyana 20
Diwali 32, 33, 44

earth, as goddess 40
ecstasy 23, 24
environment 8, 40–1, 44

equality 35
evil 14, 15, 19, 22, 30, 32

festivals 31, 32–3, 44
flood mythology 22

Gandhi, Mohandas 35, 37, 44, 45
Ganesha 11, 25
Ganga 30, 45
Ganges river 30, 31
Gayatri Mantra 28
gender equality 38–9, 44
God 8, 10, 14–17, 19, 22
    many forms of 6
    meditation on 17
    and moksha 16–17
    and murtis 29
    and pantheism 36
    revelation of 25
    see also Supreme God
goddesses 6, 8–12, 14, 22, 25, 30, 32,
    40–1
gods 6, 8–14, 25, 29–30, 32–3, 40–1
good 14, 19, 32
Gopeshwar 40
Green Pilgrimage Network 41
gurus 42

Hanuman, king of the monkeys 14, 18, 43
heaven 16
hell 16
Hindu festivals 31, 32–3, 44
Hinduism
    age of the religion 8
    and the caste system 34–5
    definition 8–9
    and dharma 18–19, 24, 25, 35–6
    diversity 6, 8–9, 25–6, 32
    and the environment 8, 40–1, 44
    and gender equality 38–9, 44
    history of 6–25
    inspiring individuals of 22–3
    in the modern world 26–45
    and moksha 16–17, 20, 24, 25, 30, 37
    and pilgrimage 30–1, 41, 44
    sacred texts 14–15
    and samsara 16, 17, 24, 25
    symbology 12–13, 25
    Vedic 6, 8–9, 28, 36
    and violence 36–7
    and world culture 42–3, 44
    and worship 14, 17, 23, 28–9, 44
    see also karma; yoga
Hindus 8, 25, 26

Indra 8, 9, 25
Indus river 8

infinity, symbols of 13
Jagannath 30, 41, 45
Jamavan, king of the bears 14
Jesus 10

Kailash, Mount 12
Kalki (a warrior on a white horse) 10, 15, 25
karma 16–17, 24, 25
    and dharma 18
    and pilgrimage 30, 44
    removal of bad 30, 31
    in Western culture 42
Kaushitaki Brahmana Upanishad 17
kavadi 33, 33, 44
Khon theatre 43
Krishna (a charioteer) 10, 15, 19, 23, 25, 36
Kshatryas (warrior caste) 34, 36
Kumbh Mela 31
Kurma (the tortoise) 10

Lakshmi 10, 12, 22, 25, 32
Lanka 14
Laws of Manu 34, 39
life stages 19
lotus flower 12

maces 12, 13
Mahabharat (Indian TV series) 42
Mahabharata 6, 14–15, 19, 24, 25, 31, 36,
    40, 42–3
mandirs 29, 44
mantras 28, 29, 42, 44
Manu 22, 25
Mata Amritanandamayi Devi 23, 25
Matsya (the fish) 10, 22
Matsya Purana 22
meditation 11, 24
    and Brahman 11
    and moksha 17
    and Shiva 12
    and yoga 20–1, 25
mind, restless 20
moksha 16–17, 20, 24, 25, 30, 37
monotheists 10, 11, 24
murtis 28–9, 30, 33, 44
Murugan 33, 45
Muslims 23
mystery 11

Nachiketas 32
Nala 14
Nandi (bull) 13
Narasimha (half man, half lion) 10
natural world 8, 40–1, 44
nirvana 17
non-violence 37, 44
numbers, sacred 29

offerings 28, 29
   see also sacrifice

pantheism 36, 37, 44
Parashurama (a great warrior) 10
parinirvana 17
Parvati 10, 11, 12, 25
Patanjali 21
patriarchal society 38, 39, 44
pilgrimage 30–1, 41, 44
polytheistic 8, 9, 10, 24
pranayama 20
puja 28, 29, 30, 44
puppets 42–3
Puranas 15, 24, 25
Puri 30, 41
Purusha 34, 45
pyres 38

Rama 10, 14, 18, 25, 32
Ramakien 43
Ramayana 6, 14, 15, 21, 24, 25, 32, 42–3,
   44
Rath Yatra 33, 44
Ravana 14, 18, 25, 32
rebirth 16
reincarnation 16–18, 17, 20, 24, 25, 32
religious tolerance 6
revelation 14, 18, 25
Rig Veda 8, 14, 28, 34, 39
Rishis 14, 15, 21, 24
rituals 14
Rudra 8, 25

sacred texts 14–15, 25
sacred thread, taking the 19
sacrifice 9, 24, 28, 36
sadhus 31
samsara 16, 17, 24, 25
sanatana dharma 19, 24
Sanskrit 8, 9, 16, 17, 20, 24
sati 38, 39, 44
Sewa UK 18
Shaivas 10, 11, 24, 25
Shankara 22–3, 25
Shiva 10, 11, 12–13, 25, 30, 33
   as Supreme God 10, 25
Shiva Purana 11
shrines, domestic 28, 38
shruti 14, 15, 24
Shudras (manual labourers/servants) 34
Sikhism 4
Sita 14, 18, 25, 32
snake symbols 13
suffering, liberation from 16
Supreme God 10, 18, 25, 29, 32–3
Supreme Goddess 11
symbols 12–13, 24, 25

tapas 20–1, 24
temples 29, 30, 44
Thaipusam 33, 44
'third eye' 12, 39
tirthas 30, 31, 44
tridents 13
Trimurti 10, 11, 24
Tripurasundari 11
trishula 13, 24

Untouchables (Dalits) 34–5
upanayana 19, 24
Upanishads 17

vahana 13, 24
Vaishnavas 10, 11, 15, 19, 23, 24, 25
Vaishyas (traders/farmers) 34
Vamana, the dwarf 10
Varaha, the boar 10
Varanasi, India 30
Vasuki, king of the serpents 13
Vedas 8, 9, 14–15, 19, 24, 25, 32, 36,
   38–9, 44
Vedic gods 8–9
Vedic Hinduism 6, 8–9, 28, 36
vibhuti 12, 13, 24
violence 36–7
Vishnu 10, 12–13, 25, 33
   avatars 10, 12, 15, 19, 22, 23, 25
   and Manu 22
   and Puri 30
   as Supreme God 10, 25
   worship 28
Vishvamitra 21, 25
Vivekananda 38

Wayang theatre 42–3
wisdom 11, 12
world culture 42–3, 44
worship 14, 17, 23, 28–9, 44

Yama 32, 45
yoga 6, 17, 20–1, 24, 25, 37, 39, 42
Yoga Sutras 21
yogins 17, 37

Acknowledgements

Every effort has been made to trace copyright holders and to obtain their permission for the use of copyright material.

The publishers will gladly receive any information enabling them to rectify any error or omission at the first opportunity.

The publishers would like to thank the following for permission to reproduce copyright material:

(t = top, b = bottom, c = centre, l = left, r = right)

Text

The Navajivan Trust for an extract by Mohandas Gandhi from The Words of Gandhi, 2001. Reproduced with permission from the Navajivan Trust, India.

Photographs

Cover and title page robert stoetzel/Alamy, pp6–7 hindu devotees Cultura RM/Alamy Stock Photo, p8 Schita/Alamy Stock Photo, p9 l Finnian M.M. Gerety, p9 r imageBroker/Alamy Stock Photo, p10 Historical Images Archive/Alamy Stock Photo, p11 t FotoFlirt/Alamy Stock Photo, p11 b Dinodia Photos/Alamy Stock Photo, p12 t Art Directors&Trip/Alamy Stock Photo, p12 b robertharding/Alamy Stock Photo, p13 laverock/Shutterstock, p14 t Universal Images Group North America LLC/Alamy Stock Photo, p14 b Heritage Image Partnership Ltd/Alamy Stock Photo, p15 Rudra Narayan Mitra/Shutterstock, p16 t Pep Roig/Alamy Stock Photo, p16 b pimpkinpie/Alamy Stock Photo, p17 Dmitry Kalinovsky/Shutterstock, p18 t Artdirectors&Trip/Alamy Stock Photo, p18 b Zuma Press, Inc./Alamy Stock Photo, p19 Roland Pargeter/Alamy Stock Photo, p20 robertharding/Alamy Stock Photo, p21 t imageBROKER/Alamy Stock Photo p21 b Dinodia Photos/Alamy Stock Photo, p22 t dinodia Photos/Alamy Stock Photo, p22 b commons.wikimedia.org, p23 t Godong/Alamy Stock Photo, p23 b Eric Fahmer/Shutterstock, pp26–27 Maciej Dakowicz/Alamy Stock Photo, p28 t Artdirectors&Trip/Alamy Stock Photo, p28 b Tim Gainey/Alamy Stock Photo, p29 saiko3p/Shutterstock, p30 t StanislavBeloglazov/Shutterstock, p30 b tantrik71/Shutterstock, p31 theaskaman306/Shutterstock, p32 Graham Oliver/Alamy Stock Photo, p33 t Calvin Chan/Shutterstock, p33 b reddees/Shutterstock, p34 Joerg Boethling/Alamy Stock Photo, p35 t Mondadori Portfolio/Getty Images, p35 b Indranil Mukherjee/AFP/Getty Images, p36 reddees/Shutterstock, p37 Hulton Archive/Getty Images, p38 Frank Bienewald/LightRocket via Getty Images, p39 Image Source Plus/Alamy Stock Photo, p40 Tim Gainey/Alamy Stock Photo, p41 t The India Today Group/Getty Images, p41 b STRDEL/AFP/Getty Images, p42 Photos 12/Alamy Stock Photo, p43 t Pacific Press/Alamy Stock Photo, p43 b K. Decha/Shutterstock, p45 t Dinodia Photos/Alamy Stock Photo, p45 b neelsky/Shutterstock.